The YOU Show

Come see how amazing you really are!

Start at the beginning, middle or end of the book; where you want to start your journaling is up to you!

There is no right or wrong way to complete this book.

Feel free to be honest when writing down your feelings, thoughts and questions!

Celebrate your uniqueness!

Name
_____

My Mixed Emotions

Learning how to recognize and show your emotions is important.

It's important to realize all emotions and feelings are important and to learn how to manage and identify them.

Here are the four main emotions:

Happiness

Anger

Fear

Sadness

All emotions have a purpose, even if they are emotions that make us feel bad.

My Hidden Emotions

Anger can be easily seen, but a lot of feelings can be hidden beneath the surface.

Loneliness

Sadness   Tiredness   Pain

Anxiety   Fear

Embarrassment

Shame   Helplessness

Hurt

Disappointment

Talking to an adult can help you find out what other feelings might be causing you to feel angry.

About Me

What I like about me:

Things I am good at:

Something I want to learn:

I am curious about:

Draw a time when you were in a good mood.

What were you doing?

What were you doing?

Draw a time when you were in a bad mood.

It's okay to have bad moods,
as long as you remember that bad moods will always
pass and good moods will always return with time.

How I Feel

Happy

I am happy when ———————————————
My thoughts are ———————————————
My body feels ———————————————

Fear

I am afraid when ———————————————
My thoughts are ———————————————
My body feels ———————————————

Sad

I am sad when ———————————————
My thoughts are ———————————————
My body feels ———————————————

Angry

I am angry when ———————————————
My thoughts are ———————————————
My body feels ———————————————

Understanding your emotions is important.
Being able to identify how you're feeling is
a key step in learning to manage your emotions.

Drawing and writing can help us reduce
stress and anxiety.
Draw a picture of your favorite place to visit.

Negative Self-Talk

When you have negative thoughts about yourself,
it can seem like they are completely true.
Try to question these negative thoughts when they happen.

Think ...

What negative thoughts do you have about yourself?
Where could these negative thoughts have come from?
Why might these negative thoughts not be true?

Write a negative thought you
have about yourself on the line.

Write a reason why this thought
may not be true on the bandage.

_____

_____

_____

_____

Color the food that best answers the question beside it.
Donuts are "Yes", French fries are "No",
and pizza slices are "Sometimes".

Yes   No   Sometimes

I am polite and respectful
to other people.

I can recognize and express
my emotions without losing
control of them.

I try to see the bright
side in every situation.

When something is hard to do,
I don't give up.

I consider how my actions and
words make other people feel.

I can keep calm
when things don't go my way.

I know when to put my
phone or tablet down.

Write one thing you sometimes worry about.

_____

Things you can do when you're worried:

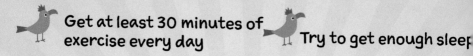

Get at least 30 minutes of exercise every day

Try to get enough sleep

Talk to an adult about your worries

Make a list of your worries

Write 3 steps you can take to help deal with your worries.

#2

#1

#3

These steps can include doing your favorite activity, making a to-do list, talking to an adult, or doing something that you find relaxing.

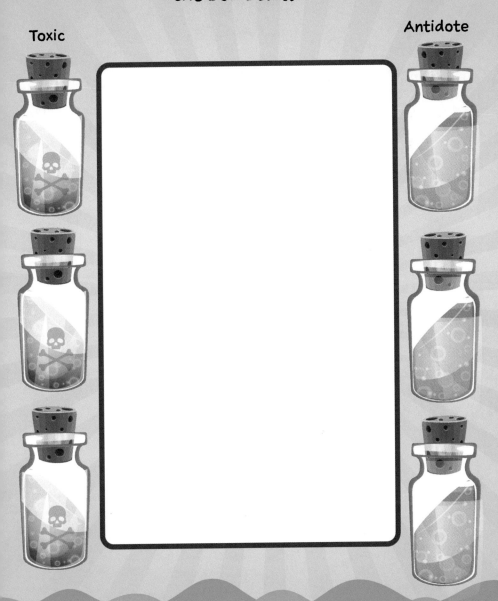

Write 3 Things that make the worry grow larger

Draw one thing that you worry about in the box below.

Write 3 Things that makes the worry feel better

Toxic

Antidote

Try to find healthy ways to cope with your worries. Writing about your worries, talking with friends and family, or doing an activity you enjoy can help you manage your worries.

Tackling Anger

What triggers anger? How does it make you feel?
How can you control it?

Trigger
Write something
that makes you angry

Body Feeling
Write how it makes the
rest of your body feel

Cool Down Plan
Write something you can
do to help calm down.

It's okay to feel angry or frustrated.
All feelings are healthy and normal parts of life!

While we can't control how we feel, we can control
what we do with those feelings. When you're angry,
try to do something positive with your anger, like
drawing a picture, punching a pillow or talking calmly
with a friend or family member.

Dealing with Sadness

Talk with someone

Take 3 deep breaths

Find a happy place

Have a good cry

Do something fun

Say calming words

Feeling sad doesn't feel nice. Always talk to someone about why you feel sad. Sometimes a change of scenery or an activity you love can help.

Weekly Emotions Diary

Monday

What upset me today:

Tuesday

What made me happy today:

Wednesday

Today I had fun when:

Thursday

Positive things I did today:

Weekly Emotions Diary

Friday

Today I had fun when:

Saturday

What made me happy today?

Sunday

Today am I grateful for?

Free Day

What I like about myself:

My Anger

Draw a picture of what you look like or how you feel when you're angry.

What do you say when you're angry?

When you are angry, how do you help yourself calm down and feel better?

ASK FOR
HELP

KNOW IT'S
OK TO
BE SAD

FOCUS
ON OTHER
THINGS

BREATHE
AND RELAX

DO THINGS
YOU LIKE

MAKE A
GRATITUDE
LIST

ENCOURAGE
YOURSELF

BE KIND
TO
YOURSELF

NAME YOUR
FEELINGS

KNOW THAT
YOU ARE AN
AMAZING
PERSON

FIND ALTERNATIVE
WAYS TO
HANDLE ANGER

FORGIVE AND
LOVE YOURSELF

Superhero

If you were a superhero, what would you look like?
What superpowers would you have?

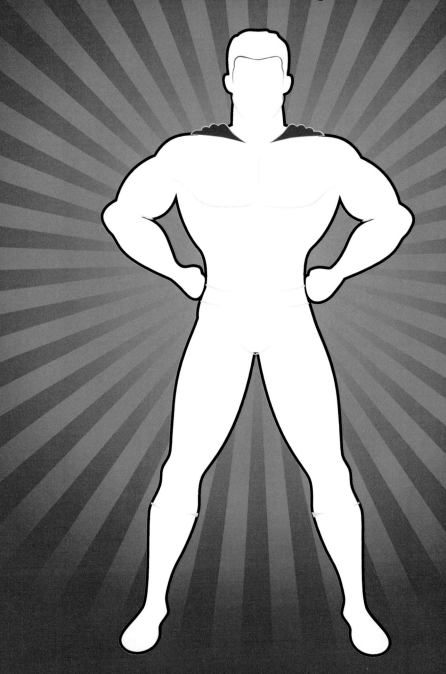

Superhero Advice

BE GRATEFUL

HELP SOMEONE IN NEED

Be Positive

BE KIND TO OTHERS

Be open-minded

Think Positive Thoughts!

Try New Things!

KEEP THE PEACE

Listen to your heart!

TURN OFF THE TV

BELIEVE IN YOURSELF

Respect yourself

It's okay to not always win.

It's okay to make mistakes

Color in the worries that you have:

Family Problems

School

Fights with Friends

Not Fitting In

Doing Poorly on Tests

Something Bad Happening

Bullying

Monsters and the Dark

Today's Affirmations
- I will not compare myself to others
- I am an amazing person
- I am smart and capable of anything I set my mind too.

For each air balloon, write a problem you have in the top box. Write a possible solution for that problem in the box below it.

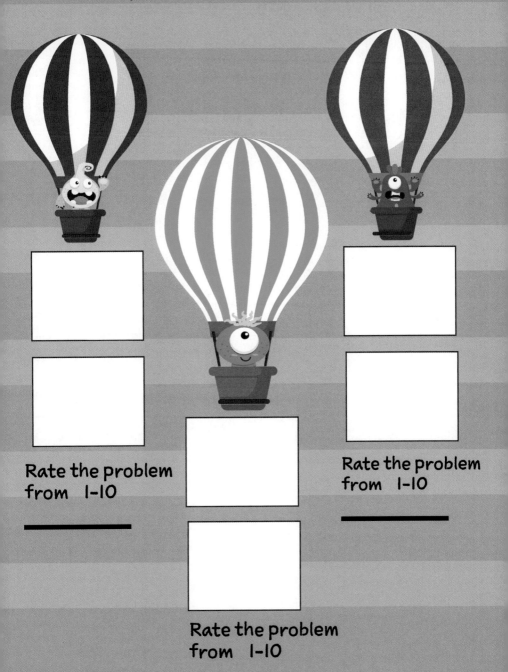

Rate the problem from 1-10

Rate the problem from 1-10

Rate the problem from 1-10

My Emotions

What emotion are you feeling?

_____
_____

Why do you think you feel this way right now?

_____
_____

What do you usually do when you feel this way?

_____
_____

What emotion are you feeling?

_____
_____

Why do you think you feel this way right now?

_____
_____

What do you usually do when you feel this way?

_____
_____

How are you feeling today? What emotions are you feeling right now?

Its not terrible to get angry or worried.
All feelings are ok!

Monster Advice

 ## Mind your manners
Always treat others the way you want to be treated: with respect and kindness.

 ## Be generous to others
Try to always lend a helping hand when someone is in need.

 ## Take responsibility for your mistakes
It's okay to make mistakes, as long as we admit to them and learn from them!

 ## Think for yourself
Follow your inner voice, instead of being vulnerable to peer pressure.

 ## Have empathy for others.
Try to imagine what it feels like to be in the other person's shoes.

My Award

Draw or write something you've accomplished
this year that makes you proud.

With hard work, courage and determination,
you can accomplish anything you set your mind to!

My Future Award

If you believe it, you can achieve it!

Draw or write one thing that you want to accomplish.

Speak Up About Your Feelings...

Open up about your feelings by writing them in
the speech and thought bubbles above.
It's important to be able to say what's on your mind

Complete The Monster Drawing

Use your imagination!

Write your worries on the baseballs.

Imagine your worries are being hit
away like a baseball being hit by a bat

Question Your Thoughts

What are you worried about?

How likely is it that your worry will come true?

If your worry does come true, what's the worst that can happen?

If your worry does come true, what's realistically most likely to happen?

If your worry comes true, will you be able to find a solution:
In one week? In one month? In one year?

I Am Unique

If you could be any person or animal for a day, who or what would you choose, and why?

Roar

What is one thing you wish you could spend more time doing? Why?

What qualities make for a good friend?

What is one thing you'd like to hear from your teacher/parent/friend?

I Am Unique

How would you like to help the world?

If you could create the perfect imaginary friend, what would they be like?

If you were going to start a business or invent a product, what would it be?

What's the most beautiful thing you have seen today/yesterday/this week?

World

Peace Day!

My Team Shirt

If you had your own sports team,
what would your shirt look like?
Draw it on the shirt above.

Write the names of the people you would choose for your sport team on the shirts below.

How do each of these people contribute to my support team?

_____
_____

_____

How do they make me feel accepted and appreciated?

_____
_____

_____

What do they bring to my world that makes me feel good?

_____
_____

_____

Anger Warning Signs

Color in the warning signs that tell you when you're angry.

My face gets hot

I raise my voice

I'm annoyed

I talk rudely to other people

I want to hit other people

I start to cry

Anger warning signs are clues that you are becoming angry. When you notice them, you can stop yourself before you lose control of your anger.

Checking Up With Myself

	Yes	No
I believe in myself		
I make wise choices		
I know that everything will eventually be okay		
I think positive thoughts		
I can be a leader		
I like who I am		
I can handle criticism		
I trust myself and my decisions		
I am happy to be me		
I love myself		
I am not afraid to try new things		
I give everything I do my all		

If you answered "No" to any of these, try to think about why you feel that way, and what you can do to make things better.

When you take the time to thank the people in your life, it can make you feel better, while helping others feel appreciated.
Who are you grateful for?

To _____

THANK YOU

for

_____
_____
_____

To _____

THANK YOU

for

_____
_____
_____

One experience I am grateful for:

_____

_____

_____

One kind thing someone has done for me:

_____

_____

_____

Write what you are grateful for today on the planets.

My Worry Shield

Draw a design on the shield that represents who you are, your interests, and what you are good at.

WARRIOR

Name —————————————————————

Worries can grow stronger if you focus on negative thoughts. Remembering who you are and focusing on your positive qualities can help you feel stronger than your worries!

Color In your Strengths

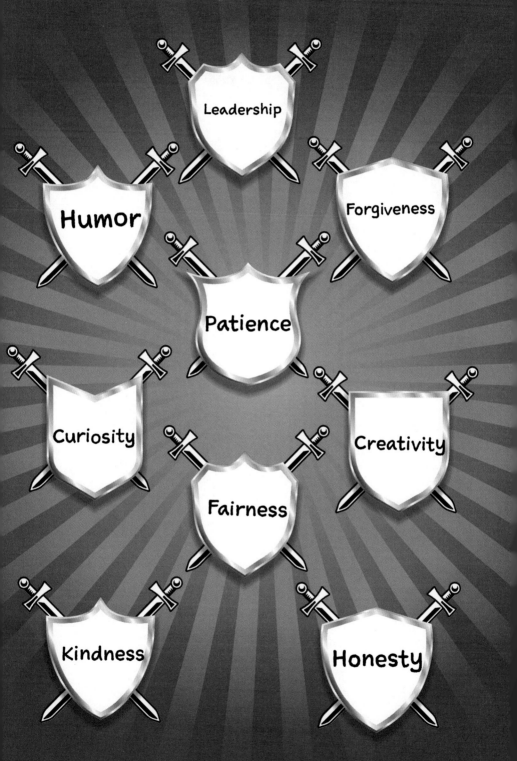

Imagine you are on your dream trip to anywhere in the world. What would your dream trip look like? Where would you go? What would your postcard say? Who would you send it to?

Let's go on a
ADVENTURE

POSTCARD

to:

from:

Design your ship for your adventure

Yours Truly

Imagine you are meeting someone for the first time.
What are three things about yourself that they should know

1.
_____

2.
_____

3.
_____

What is one thing I am looking forward to?

_____

Who is someone I am grateful for?

_____

What is my favorite memory?

_____

Keep Being You!

Three things I like to do by myself:

1. _____

2. _____

3. _____

Do you have any nicknames? If so, what are they?

_____

What do I like most about myself?

_____

Which three words describe me best?

_____

If I were a fruit, what fruit would I be?

_____

Happy Birthday to Me!

Draw a picture or write about what your dream present to yourself would be.

Decorate your birthday socks

I Am Awesome

In this world, there is only one you.
Draw your unique self below.

Believe In Yourself

Your thoughts and beliefs are powerful.
Positive thinking can help positively
shape the world around you.

What have you accomplished
by believing in yourself?

_____ _____

_____ _____

No matter what others think, it is important to always
believe in yourself.

Be your own
best friend

Respect
yourself

Don't put
yourself
down

Recognize
your
strengths

Have faith
in your
abilities

Why am I Fortunate?

Write reasons why you're fortunate on the coins.

My Message

If you were leaving a message in a time capsule
for someone ten years in the future to find, what would you say?

My Feelings

Look at the emotions written on the pizza slices below.
Write on the pizza slices something that has happened in
your life that has made you feel each emotion.

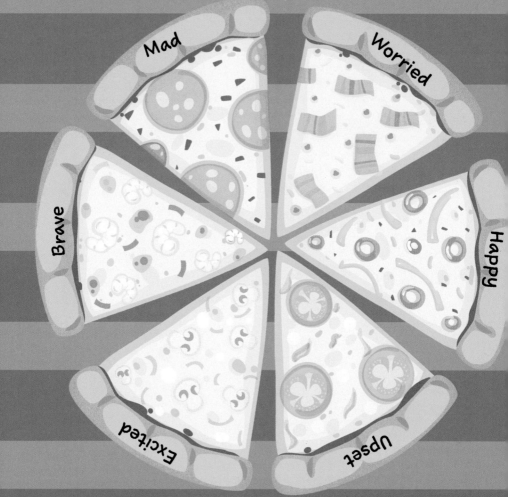

Mad

Worried

Brave

Happy

Excited

Upset

When I Am Upset, I Can ...

- Take 10 deep breaths
- Listen to music
- Paint or draw
- Go for a walk
- Play a sport
- Hug someone
- Talk to a friend
- Have alone time
- Dance or sing

My Best Mistakes

Write down a mistake you have made before on each of the eggs.

Write one thing you learned from each mistake on the bacon strips.

REMEMBER

. Mistakes help you develop problem solving skills

. Mistakes build character

. Mistakes help you learn what works and what doesn't work

Imagine if you had the power to become invisible
whenever and wherever you wanted.
What would you do with this power?

What do you think the hardest job in the world is? Why?

When you're in a bad mood, what helps you to feel better?

If you could have the best day ever, what would you do?
Where would you go? Who would you spend the day with?

My Family

Draw a picture of your family in the big picture frame.
In the other picture frames, write or draw your favorite
memories that you have with your family.

Tell someone in your family that
you love them today!

My Story

If you had a book that told the story of your life,
what would the cover of the book look like?
Draw the cover of your life story below.

Write a story about your future self

Feel free to tell your future self about your goals,
hopes, fears and dreams.

My Future Self

_____

_____

_____

_____

_____

_____

_____

_____

_____

_____

_____

_____

_____

Made in the USA
Columbia, SC
22 January 2020